Johnny Appleseed

JOHNNY APPLESEED

A PIONEER HERO

by W. D. Haley

as first published in
Harper's Monthly Magazine, 1871

CHAPMAN BILLIES, INC.
Sandwich, Massachusetts

First published in Harper's Monthly Magazine,
No. 258, November, 1871.

This edition published in 1994 by
Chapman Billies, Inc.
P.O. Box 819
Sandwich, Massachusetts 02563

ISBN: 0–939218–04–6

First Edition
Printed in the United States of America

for
Christopher, Jordan, Molly, and Jacob

JOHNNY APPLESEED
A Pioneer Hero

THE FAR WEST is rapidly becoming only a traditional designation; railroads have destroyed the romance of frontier life, or have surrounded it with so many appliances of civilization that the pioneer character is rapidly becoming mythical. The men and women who obtain their groceries and dry goods from New York by rail in a few hours have nothing in common with those who, fifty years ago, "packed salt" a hundred miles to make their mush palatable, and could only exchange corn and wheat for molasses and calico by making long and perilous voyages in flat boats down the Ohio and Mississippi rivers to New Orleans.* Two generations of frontier lives have accumulated stores of narrative which, like the

---

* The reader is reminded that this was written in 1871.

small-but-beautiful tributaries of great rivers, are forgotten in the broad sweep of the larger current of history. The march of Titans sometimes tramples out the memory of smaller but more useful lives, and sensational glare often eclipses more modest but purer lights. This has been the case in the popular demand for the dime novel dilutions of James Fenimore Cooper's romances of border life, which have preserved the records of Indian rapine and atrocity as the only memorials of pioneer history. But the early days of western settlement witnessed sublimer heroisms than those of human torture, and nobler victories than those of the tomahawk and scalping knife.

Among the heroes of endurance that was voluntary, and of action that was creative and not sanguinary, there was one man whose name, seldom mentioned now save by some of the few surviving pioneers, deserves to be perpetuated.

The first reliable trace of our modest hero finds him in the Territory of Ohio, in 1801, with a horse load of apple seeds, which he planted in various places on and about the borders of Licking Creek, the first orchard thus originated by him being on the farm of Isaac Stadden, in what is now known as Licking County, in the State of Ohio. During the five succeeding years, although he was undoubtedly following the same strange occupation, we have no authentic account of his movements until we reach a pleasant spring day in 1806, when a pioneer settler in Jefferson County, Ohio, noticed a peculiar craft, with a remarkable occupant and a curious cargo, slowly dropping down with the current of the Ohio River. It was "Johnny Appleseed," by which name Jonathan Chapman was afterward known in every log cabin from the Ohio River to the northern lakes, and westward to the prairies of what is now the State of Indiana. With two canoes lashed together he was transporting a load of apple seeds to the western frontier, for the purpose of creating orchards on the farthest verge of white settlements. With his canoes he passed down the Ohio to Marietta, where he entered the Muskingum, ascending the stream of that river until he reached the mouth of the Walhonding, or White Woman Creek, and still onward, up the Mohican, into the Black Fork, to the head of navigation, in the region now known as Ashland and Richland counties, on the line of the Pittsburgh and Fort Wayne Railroad, in Ohio. A long and toilsome voyage it was, as a glance at the map will show, and must have occupied a great deal of time, as the lonely traveler stopped at every inviting spot to plant the seeds and make his infant nurseries. These are the first well-authenticated facts in the history of Jonathan Chapman, whose birth, there is good reason for believing, occurred in Boston, Massachusetts, in 1775. According to this, which was his own statement in one of his less reticent moods, he was, at the time of his appearance on Licking Creek, twenty-six years of age, and whether impelled in his eccentricities by some absolute misery of the heart which could only find relief in incessant motion, or governed by a benevolent monomania, his whole afterlife was devoted to the work of planting apple seeds in remote places. The seeds he gathered from the cider presses of western Pennsylvania; but his canoe voyage in 1806 appears to have been the only occasion upon which he adopted that method of transporting them, as all his subsequent journeys were made on foot. Having planted his stock of seeds, he would return to Pennsylvania for a fresh supply, and, as sacks made of any less substantial fabric would not endure the hard usage of the long trip through forests dense with underbrush and briers, he provided himself with leathern bags. Securely packed, the seeds were conveyed, sometimes on the back of a horse, and not infrequently on his own shoulders, either over a part of the old Indian trail that led from Fort Duquesne to Detroit, by way of Fort Saudusky, or over what is styled in the appendix to Hutchins's History of

Boguet's Expedition in 1764 the "second route through the wilderness of Ohio," which would require him to traverse a distance of one hundred and sixty-six miles in a west-northwest direction from Fort Duquesne in order to reach the Black Fork of the Mohican.

This region, although it is now densely populated, still possesses a romantic beauty that railroads and bustling towns can not obliterate — a country of forest-clad hills and green valleys, through which numerous bright streams flow on their way to the Ohio; but when Johnny Appleseed reached some lonely log cabin he would find himself in a veritable wilderness. The old settlers say that the margins of the streams, near which the first settlements were generally made, were thickly covered with a low, matted growth of small timber, while nearer to the water was a rank mass of long grass, interlaced with morning glory and wild pea vines, among which funereal willows and clustering alders stood like sentinels on the outpost of civilization. The hills, that rise almost to the dignity of mountains, were crowned with forest trees, and in the coverts were innumerable bears, wolves, deer, and droves of wild hogs, that were as ferocious as any beast of prey. In the grass, the massasauga and other venomous reptiles lurked in such numbers that a settler named Chandler has left the fact on record that during the first season of his residence, while mowing a little prairie which formed part of his land, he killed over two hundred black rattlesnakes in an area that would involve an average destruction of one of these reptiles for each rod of land. The frontiersman, who felt himself sufficiently protected by his rifle against wild beasts and hostile Indians, found it necessary to guard against the attacks of the insidious enemies in the grass by wrapping bandages of dried grass around his buckskin leggings and moccasins; but Johnny would shoulder his bag of apple seeds, and with bare feet penetrate to some remote spot that combined picturesqueness and fertility of soil, and there he would plant his seeds, place a slight enclosure around the place, and leave them to grow until the trees were large enough to be transplanted by the settlers, who, in the mean time, would have made their clearings in the vicinity. The sites chosen by him are, many of them, well known, and are such as an artist or a poet would select—open places on the loamy lands that border the creeks—rich, secluded spots, hemmed in by giant trees, picturesque now, but fifty years ago, with their wild surroundings and the primal silence, they must have been ten-fold more so. In personal appearance, Chapman was a small, wiry man, full of restless activity; he had long dark hair, a scanty beard that was never shaved, and keen black eyes that sparkled with a peculiar brightness. His dress was of the oddest description. Generally, even in the coldest weather, he went barefooted, but sometimes, for his long journeys, he would make himself a rude pair of sandals; at other times he would wear any cast-off foot covering he chanced to find—a boot on one foot and an old brogan or a moccasin on the other. It appears to have been a matter of conscience with him never to purchase shoes, although he was rarely without money enough to do so. On one occasion, in an unusually cold November, while he was traveling barefooted through mud and snow, a settler who happened to possess a pair of shoes that were too small for his own use forced their acceptance upon Johnny, declaring that it was sinful for a human being to travel with naked feet in such weather. A few days afterward, the donor was in the village that has since become the thriving city of Mansfield and met his beneficiary contentedly plodding along with his feet bare and half frozen. With some degree of anger he inquired for the cause of such foolish conduct, and received for reply that Johnny had overtaken a poor, barefooted family moving westward, and as they appeared to be in much greater need of clothing than he was, he had given them the shoes. His dress was generally composed of cast-off clothing, that he had taken in payment for apple trees; and as the pioneers were far less extravagant than their descendants in such matters, the homespun and buckskin garments that they discarded would not be very elegant or serviceable. In his later years, however, he seems to have thought that even this kind of second-hand raiment was too luxurious, as his principal garment was made of a coffee sack, in which he cut holes for his head and arms to pass through, and pronounced it "a very serviceable cloak, and as good clothing as any man need wear." In the matter of headgear his taste was equally unique; his first experiment was with a tin vessel that served to cook his mush, but this was open to the objection that it did not protect his eyes from the beams of the sun; so he construct-ed a hat of pasteboard with an immense peak in front, and having thus secured an article that combined usefulness with economy, it became his permanent fashion. Thus strangely clad, he was perpetually wandering through forests and morasses, and suddenly appearing in white settlements and Indian villages; but there must have been some rare force of gentle goodness dwelling in his looks and breathing in his words, for it is the testimony of all who knew him that, notwithstanding his ridiculous attire, he was always treated with the greatest respect by the rudest frontiersman, and, what is a better test, the boys of the settlements forbore to jeer at him. With grown-up people and boys he was usually reticent, but manifested great affection for little girls, always having pieces of ribbon and gay calico to give to his little favorites. Many a grandmother in Ohio and Indiana can remember the presents she received when a child from poor homeless Johnny Appleseed. When he consented to eat with any family he would never sit down to the table until he was assured that there was an ample supply for the children; and his sympathy for their youthful troubles and his kindness toward them made him friends among all the juveniles of the borders.

The Indians also treated Johnny with the greatest kindness. By these wild and sanguinary savages he was regarded as a "great medicine man," on account of his strange appearance, eccentric actions, and, especially, the fortitude with which he could endure pain, in proof of which he would often thrust pins and needles into his flesh. His nervous sensibilities really seem to have been less acute than those of ordinary people, for his method of treating the cuts and sores that were the consequences of his barefooted wanderings through briers and thorns was to sear the wound with a red-hot iron, and then cure the burn. During the war of 1812, when the frontier settlers were tortured and slaughtered by the savage allies of Great Britain, Johnny Appleseed continued his wanderings, and was never harmed by the roving bands of hostile Indians. On many occasions the

The tribes of the heathen are round about your doors,
and a devouring flame followeth after them.

impunity with which he ranged the country enabled him to give the settlers warning of approaching danger in time to allow them to take refuge in their blockhouses before the savages could attack them. Our informant refers to one of these instances, when the news of Hull's surrender came like a thunderbolt upon the frontier. Large bands of Indians and British were destroying everything before them and murdering defenseless women and children, and even the blockhouses were not always a sufficient protection. At this time, Johnny traveled day and night, warning the people of the approaching danger. He visited every cabin and delivered this message: "The Spirit of the Lord is upon me, and he hath anointed me to blow the trumpet in the wilderness, and sound an alarm in the forest; for, behold, the tribes of the heathen are round about your doors, and a devouring flame followeth after them." The aged man who narrated this incident said that he could feel even now the thrill that was caused by this prophetic announcement of the wild-looking herald of danger, who aroused the family on a bright moonlit midnight with his piercing voice. Refusing all offers of food and denying himself a moment's rest, he traversed the border day and night until he had warned every settler of the approaching peril.

His diet was as meager as his clothing. He believed it to be a sin to kill any creature for food, and thought that all that was necessary for human sustenance was produced by the soil. He was also a strenuous opponent of the waste of food, and on one occasion, on approaching a log cabin, he observed some fragments of bread floating on the surface of a bucket of slops that was intended for the pigs. He immediately fished them out, and when the housewife expressed her astonishment, he told her that it was an abuse of the gifts of a merciful God to allow the smallest quantity of any thing that was designed to supply the wants of mankind to be diverted from its purpose.

In this instance, as in his whole life, the peculiar religious ideas of Johnny Appleseed were exemplified. He was a most earnest disciple of the faith taught by Emanuel Swedenborg, and himself claimed to have frequent conversations with angels and spirits; two of the latter, of the feminine gender, he asserted, had revealed to him that they were to be his wives in a future state if he abstained from a matrimonial alliance on earth. He entertained a profound reverence for the revelations of the Swedish seer, and always carried a few old volumes with him. These he was very anxious should be read by everyone, and he was probably not only the first colporteur in the wilderness of Ohio, but as he had no tract society to furnish him supplies, he certainly devised an original method of multiplying one book into a number. He divided his books into several pieces, leaving a portion at a log cabin, and on a subsequent visit furnishing another fragment, and continuing this process as diligently as though the work had been

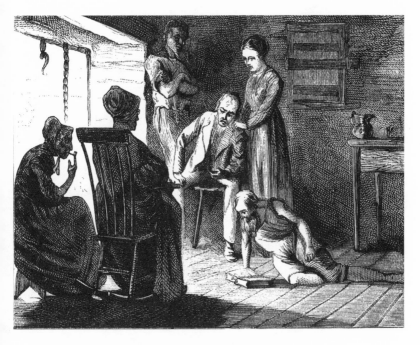

News right fresh from heaven

published in serial numbers. By this plan he was enabled to furnish reading for several people at the same time, and out of one book; but it must have been a difficult undertaking for some nearly illiterate backwoodsman to endeavor to comprehend Swedenborg by a backward course of reading, when his first installment happened to be the last fraction of the volume. Johnny's faith in Swedenborg's works was so reverential as almost to be superstitious. He was once asked if, in traveling barefooted through forests abounding with venomous reptiles, he was not afraid of being bitten. With his peculiar smile, he drew his book from his bosom, and said, "This book is an infallible protection against all danger here and hereafter."

It was his custom, when he had been welcomed to some hospitable log house after a weary day of journeying, to lie down on the puncheon floor, and, after inquiring if his auditors would hear "some news right fresh from heaven," produce his few tattered books, among which would be a New Testament, and read and expound until his uncultivated hearers would catch the spirit and glow of his enthusiasm, while they scarcely comprehended his language. A lady who knew him in his later years writes in the following terms of one of these domiciliary readings of poor, self-sacrificing Johnny Appleseed: "We can hear him read now, just as he did that summer day, when we were busy quilting upstairs, and he lay near the door, his voice rising denunciatory and thrilling — strong and loud as the roar of wind and waves, then soft and soothing as the balmy airs that quivered the morning glory leaves about his gray beard. His was a strange eloquence at times, and he was undoubtedly a man of genius." What a scene is presented to our imagination! The interior of a primitive cabin, the wide, open fireplace, where a few sticks are burning beneath the iron pot in which the evening meal is cooking; around the fireplace the attentive group, composed of the sturdy pioneer and his wife and children, listening with a reverential awe to the "news right fresh from heaven"; and reclining on the floor, clad in rags, but with his gray hairs glorified by the beams of the setting sun that flood through the open door and the unchinked logs of the humble building, this poor wanderer, with the gift of genius and eloquence, who believes with the faith of apostles and martyrs that God has appointed him a mission in the wilderness to preach the Gospel of love, and plant apple seeds that shall produce orchards for the benefit of men and women and little children whom he has never seen. If there is a sublimer faith or a more genuine eloquence in richly decorated cathedrals and under brocade vestments, it would be worth a long journey to find it.

Next to his advocacy of his peculiar religious ideas, his enthusiasm for the cultivation of apple trees in what he termed "the only proper way"— that is, from the seed — was the absorbing object of his life. Upon this, as upon religion, he was elo-

quent in his appeals. He would describe the grow-
ing and ripening fruit as such a rare and beautiful
gift of the Almighty with words that became
pictures, until his hearers could almost see its
manifold forms of beauty present before them. To
his eloquence on this subject, as well as to his
actual labors in planting nurseries, the country
over which he traveled for so many years is
largely indebted for its numerous orchards. But
he denounced as absolute wickedness all devices
of pruning and grafting, and would speak of the
act of cutting a tree as if it were a cruelty inflicted
upon a sentient being.

Not only is he entitled to the fame of being the
earliest colporteur on the frontiers, but in the
work of protecting animals from abuse and suffer-
ing he preceded, while, in his smaller sphere, he
equaled the zeal of the good Mr. Bergh. Whenever
Johnny saw an animal abused, or heard of it, he
would purchase it and give it to some more
humane settler, on condition that it should be

kindly treated and properly cared for. It frequently happened that the long journey into the wilderness would cause the new settlers to be encum-
bered with lame and broken-down horses, that
were turned loose to die. In the autumn Johnny
would make a diligent search for all such animals,
and, gathering them up, he would bargain for
their food and shelter until the next spring, when
he would lead them away to some good pasture
for the summer. If they recovered so as to be capa-
ble of working, he would never sell them, but
would lend or give them away, stipulating for their
good usage. His conception of the absolute sin of
inflicting pain or death upon any creature was not
limited to the higher forms of animal life, but
everything that had being was to him, in the fact
of its life, endowed with so much of the Divine
Essence that to wound or destroy it was to inflict
an injury upon some atom of Divinity. No Brah-
min could be more concerned for the preservation
of insect life, and the only occasion on which he

destroyed a venomous reptile was a source of long regret, to which he could never refer without manifesting sadness. He had selected a suitable place for planting apple seeds on a small prairie, and in order to prepare the ground he was mowing the long grass, when he was bitten by a rattlesnake. In describing the event, he sighed heavily, and said, "Poor fellow, he only just touched me, when I, in the heat of my ungodly passion, put the heel of my scythe in him and went away. Some time afterward I went back, and there lay the poor fellow dead." Numerous anecdotes bearing upon his respect for every form of life are preserved and form the staple of pioneer recollections. On one occasion, a cool autumnal night, when Johnny, who always camped out in preference to sleeping in a house, had built a fire near which he intended to pass the night, he noticed that the blaze attracted large numbers of mosquitoes, many of whom flew too near to his fire and were burned. He immediately brought water and quenched the

fire, accounting for his conduct afterward by say-
ing, "God forbid that I should build a fire for my
comfort which should be the means of destroying
any of His creatures!" At another time, he removed the fire he had built near a hollow log and
slept on the snow, because he found that the log
contained a bear and her cubs, whom, he said, he
did not wish to disturb. And this unwillingness to
inflict pain or death was equally strong when he
was a sufferer by it, as the following will show.
Johnny had been assisting some settlers to make a
road through the woods, and in the course of their
work they accidentally destroyed a hornets' nest.
One of the angry insects soon found a lodgment
under Johnny's coffee-sack cloak, but although it
stung him repeatedly he removed it with the
greatest gentleness. The men who were present
laughingly asked him why he did not kill it. To
which he gravely replied that, "It would not be
right to kill the poor thing, for it did not intend to
hurt me."

Theoretically he was as methodical in matters of business as any merchant. In addition to their picturesqueness, the locations of his nurseries were all fixed with a view to a probable demand for the trees by the time they had attained sufficient growth for transplanting. He would give them away to those who could not pay for them. Generally, however, he sold them for old clothing or a supply of corn meal; but he preferred to receive a note payable at some indefinite period. When this was accomplished, he seemed to think that the transaction was completed in a business-like way; but if the giver of the note did not attend to its payment, the holder of it never troubled himself about its collection. His expenses for food and clothing were so very limited that, notwithstanding his freedom from the auri sacra fames, he was frequently in possession of more money than he cared to keep, and it was quickly disposed of for wintering infirm horses, or given to some poor family whom the ague had prostrated or the accidents of border life impoverished. In a single instance only is he known to have invested his surplus means in the purchase of land, having received a deed from Alexander Finley, of Mohican Township, Ashland County, Ohio, for a part of the southwest quarter of section twenty-six; but with his customary indifference to matters of value, Johnny failed to record the deed and lost it. Only a few years ago the property was in litigation.

We must not leave the reader under the impression that this man's life, so full of hardship and perils, was a gloomy or unhappy one. There is an element of human pride in all martyrdom, which, if it does not soften the pains, stimulates the power of endurance. Johnny's life was made serenely happy by the conviction that he was living like the primitive Christians. Nor was he devoid of a keen humor, to which he occasionally gave vent, as the following will show. Toward the latter part of Johnny's career in Ohio, an itinerant missionary found his way to the village of Mansfield and preached to an open-air congregation. The discourse was tediously lengthy, and unnecessarily severe upon the sin of extravagance, which was beginning to manifest itself among the pioneers by an occasional indulgence in the carnal vanities of calico and "store tea." There was a good deal of the Pharisaic leaven in the preacher, who very frequently emphasized his discourse by the inquiry, "Where now is there a man who, like the primitive Christians, is traveling to heaven barefooted and clad in coarse raiment?" When this interrogation had been repeated beyond all reasonable endurance, Johnny rose from the log on which he was reclining, and advancing to the speaker, he placed one of his bare feet upon the stump which served for a pulpit, and pointing to his coffee-sack garment, he quietly said, "Here's your primitive Christian!" The well-clothed missionary hesitated and stammered and dismissed the congregation. His pet antithesis was destroyed by Johnny's personal appearance, which was far more primitive than the preacher cared to copy. Some of the pioneers were disposed to think that Johnny's humor was the cause of an extensive practical joke; but it is generally conceded now that a wide-spread annoyance was really the result of his belief that the offensively odored weed known in the West as the dog fennel, but more generally styled the Mayweed, possessed valuable antimalarial virtues. He procured some seeds of the plant in Pennsylvania, and sowed them in the vicinity of every house in the region of his travels. The consequence was that successive flourishing crops of the weed spread over the whole country and caused almost as much trouble as the disease it was intended to ward off; and to this day the dog fennel, introduced by Johnny Appleseed, is one of the worst grievances of the Ohio farmers.

In 1838—thirty-seven years after his appearance on Licking Creek—Johnny noticed that civilization, wealth, and population were pres-

Here's your primitive Christian

sing into the wilderness of Ohio. Hitherto he had easily kept just in advance of the wave of settlement; but now towns and churches were making their appearance, and even, at long intervals, the stage-driver's horn broke the silence of the grand old forests, and he felt that his work was done in the region in which he had labored so long. He visited every house, and took a solemn farewell of all the families. The little girls who had been delighted with his gifts of fragments of calico and ribbons had become sober matrons, and the boys who had wondered at his ability to bear the pain caused by running needles into his flesh were heads of families. With parting words of admonition, he left them and turned his steps steadily toward the setting sun.

During the succeeding nine years he pursued his eccentric avocation on the western border of Ohio and in Indiana. In the summer of 1847, when his labors had literally borne fruit over a hundred thousand square miles of territory, at the close of a warm day, after traveling twenty miles, he entered the house of a settler in Allen County, Indiana, and was, as usual, warmly welcomed. He declined to eat with the family but accepted some bread and milk, which he partook of sitting on the doorstep and gazing on the setting sun. Later in the evening he delivered his "news right fresh from heaven" by reading the Beatitudes. Declining other accommodation, he slept, as usual, on the floor, and in the early morning he was found with his features all aglow with a supernal light, and his body so near death that his tongue refused its office. The physician, who was hastily summoned, pronounced him dying, but added that he had never seen a man in so placid a state at the approach of death. At seventy-two years of age, forty-six of which had been devoted to his self-imposed mission, he ripened into death as naturally and beautifully as the seeds of his own planting had grown into fiber and bud and blossom and the matured fruit.

Thus died one of the memorable men of pioneer times, who never inflicted pain or knew an enemy — a man of strange habits, in whom there dwelt a comprehensive love that reached with one hand downward to the lowest forms of life and with the other upward to the very throne of God. A laboring, self-denying benefactor of his race, homeless, solitary, and ragged, he trod the thorny earth with bare and bleeding feet, intent only upon making the wilderness fruitful. Now "no man knoweth of his sepulchre"; but his deeds will live in the fragrance of the apple blossoms he loved so well, and the story of his life, however crudely narrated, will be a perpetual proof that true heroism, pure benevolence, noble virtues, and deeds that de- serve immortality may be found under meanest apparel and far from, gilded halls and towering spires.

COLOPHON

Johnny Appleseed, A Pioneer Hero was designed at The Philidor Company in Boston by Scott-Martin Kosofsky. The text type is Fairfield, created for the Linotype Company in the late 1930's by Rudolph Ruzicka. The version used here was skillfully adapted for PostScript imaging by Alex Kaczun, again for Linotype. The heads are set in Rudolf Koch's Koch-Antiqua, issued by the Klingspor Foundry between 1922–1924.

The four wood engravings were scanned from the original edition of the story, published by Harper's Monthly Magazine in 1871.

The book was printed and bound by BookCrafters, Inc.